THE 2,466-YEAR-OLD CALENDAR

NOBODY COULD SEE

THE 2,466-YEAR-OLD CALENDAR NOBODY COULD SEE

By Mary E. Lewis

Edition 3

Revised Jan and Feb 2018

ISBN-13:978-1542306317
ISBN-10: 1542306310

The Word of YHVH Bible is used for all Scripture references except where otherwise noted

Images and tables by © Mary E. Lewis

1—THE BIBLE'S CALENDAR TO THE END

Keep in mind that any calendar is merely a tool to aid in understanding and recording history and equally important in understanding Bible times and timing.

Just so you will know, I am not trying to fool anyone. The Bible really does have a calendar that has been overlooked as an official active full-time calendar to the end of Daniel's seventy sevens prophecy. There is not one vacuum of time in this calendar; there is no unaccounted-for gap between Jesus' ascension and his return.

Frankly, I always thought it boring to study Old Testament chronologies. I discovered the importance of them when I decided to do this book to determine the correct beginning date for Daniel's seventy-sevens. It was a real challenge, but well worth it. I refer to this booklet often to clarify other things in the Bible. I believe it is a necessary handbook for serious Bible study and historical studies.

It will be fully explained throughout this booklet, during which time, the Bible will expose the doctrines that have impeded full knowledge of this calendar. Hopefully, the error of those doctrines will become evident to those who know or practice them.

Apostle Paul very aptly described the purpose of YaHavah's Bible calendar.

Acts 17:24-28—*24*—*YHVH that made the world and all things therein, seeing that he is Lord of heaven and earth, dwells not in temples made with hands. 25—neither is worshipped with men's hands, as though he needed anything, seeing he gives to all life, and breath, and all things. 26—and has made of one blood all nations of men to dwell on all the face of the earth, **and has***

1

determined the times before appointed, and the boundaries of their circumstance. ²⁷*that they should seek the Lord, if deciding they might search for him, and find him, though he is not far from every one of us:* ²⁸*for in him we live, and move, and have our being; as certain also of your own poets have said, for we are also his offspring.*

YaHavah's Bible calendar to the end is his appointed times and the boundaries of their circumstance.

Here is a sneak-peek of what the long lost and fleshed-out calendar looks like. The full description is in section 6—*Begin the Seventy-weeks.*

- Begin counting when Cyrus decreed to rebuild the temple in AM 3932

- Jesus birth AM 4382
- Baptized AM 4412
  ○ End of 62 weeks
- Jesus' death, resurrection, and ascension AM 4415

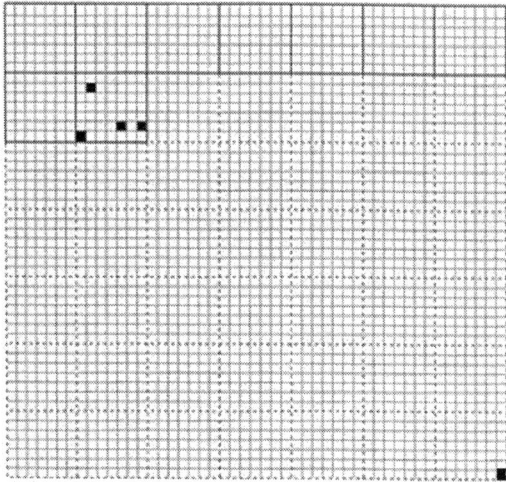

Year AM 6381 (2000 AD)

The last seven years of each succeeding block of 49 years is the potential last seven years of Daniel's seventy sevens prophecy.

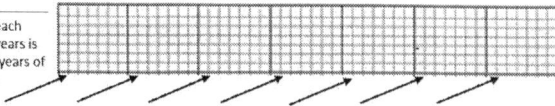

The calendar began at the end of Jerusalem's Babylonian captivity, but to know the biblical year it began, one must go back to the beginning in Adam's time.

The Bible's calendar is about YaHavah's timing and prophecy or people and events he has foretold. The calendar is linear; counting the years from Adam forward without any lapses or gaps. It progresses in two stages. The first is a Bible chronology filtered through YaHavah's righteous line in Jesus' genealogy to Jerusalem's Babylonian captivity. The second stage is Daniel's seventy sevens prophecy to the end.

To avoid being caught in Satan's diversionary tactics; know with certainty that there is only one line of history of which Christians must be fully aware. It is YaHavah's line of history in his calendar of Bible time fully reported within the pages of the Bible.

What about other calendars?

This booklet is a condensed version of YaHavah's Bible calendar. The accepted reference for linear Bible dating is AM or A.M., which refers to Anno Mundi, Latin for the *year of the world or creation.* In this case, it is *the creation of man.* The count of years is from Adam forward in a linear format.

The Gregorian calendar utilizes AD and BC to designate the years before or after Christ. AD or A.D. commonly refers to Anno Domini, Latin for *in the Year of (Our) Lord.* AD is applied to years following 1 BC in the Julian and Gregorian calendars. BC or B.C. refers to *before Christ,* an epoch used in dating years prior to the estimated birth of Jesus used in the Julian and Gregorian calendars. There are no zero years. This dating system was devised in 525 AD but was not widely used until after 800 AD. (Wikipedia article titled Anno Domini)

Other designations are ACE for after the Common Era and BCE for before the Common Era. Please understand, there is nothing common about Jesus Christ.

Calculating BC dates is worked backward from the birth of Christ. Unfortunately, not all dates agree, not even the year of Jesus's birth. My point here is that dates in the *Common Era time* or *linear time* are only general tools to help us along the road of history and truth. As with any calendar attempting to put dates to ancient history, it is well to remember that even Bible linear years can be off, plus or minus, though usually within a very small range. Focusing on dates can put the big picture out of focus.

Theologians and historians have divided Bible time into dispensations.

> *In human understanding, the label "dispensationalism" is derived from the idea that Biblical history is best understood through division into a series of chronologically successive dispensations.* (The free dictionary by Farlex; Toshiba Edition, 2016 "Dispensationalism")

Dispensationalism in Christian Theology is a type of chronology for historical biblical progression.

From the worldview, the most straightforward stages (dispensations, if you prefer) are described in these seven designations recognized as the classical dispensations.

1. Innocence (Genesis 1-2) —Adam and Eve before they sinned
2. Conscience (Genesis 3-8) — First sin to the flood
3. Civil Government (Genesis 9-11) — After the flood, government
4. Promise (Genesis 12-Ex. 19) — Abraham to Moses, the Law is given
5. Law (Exodus 20-Acts 2:4) — Moses to the cross
6. Grace (Acts 2:4—Revelation 20:3) — Cross to the millennial kingdom
7. Millennial Kingdom (Rev. 20:4-6) — The rule of Christ on earth in the millennial kingdom

Daniel was the bridge between the end of Judah's captivity and the beginning of the Bible's calendar. Daniel's four beasts are critical in the transition from the captivity to the beginning of the calendar and at its end.

Most theologians refer to the times we are in as the *end times* and *dispensations*; however, Jesus referred to the *age* we are in as *this generation*. That term has confused many Bible students. Was he talking about a 40 or 60-year duration or was it broader in scope? The word *dispensation* is not in the Bible and has also caused some confusion.

Human life began with Adam; therefore, the word *generations* is more descriptive of Adam's lost relationship with YaHavah and the struggles of humanity in regaining it. Looking at life on this earth as generations from that perspective, we can see that there are only three *generations* of humanity in the Bible:

1. The **first generation** of humanity began with Adam and ended with the Great Flood leaving only Noah and his family to fill the earth again (1,657 years from Adam). They had only *conscience* to measure good and evil. The righteous people in the first generation passed on their knowledge of the Almighty Creator. The unrighteous fought against that knowledge.

2. The **second generation** began with Noah and his sons and ended in the Babylonian captivity (2,275 years from the Flood). During this generation, the Law was introduced during the Wilderness Journey of the twelve tribes of Israel (Jacob). Their journey began after escaping from Egypt. The second generation was under Old Testament Covenant *Law* to measure good and evil.

3. The **third generation** is in the total seventy sevens calendar, that began at the end of the Babylonian captivity of Jerusalem. It is the generation or age

5

Jesus meant when he said, *"In truth, I say to you, This generation shall not pass, till all these things be fulfilled."* (Mark 13:30)

We are now in 2017 AD; which is 2,466 years from the first year of Cyrus (one of the three kings of Daniel's second beast called the bear) and counting. The year 2017 AD is 6,398 years from Adam or AM 6398. The third generation is under grace and the anointing of the Spirit of YaHavah through Jesus Christ. It is a proving time for humanity to accept or reject the Son of YaHavah for salvation from YaHavah's wrath or destruction by his wrath.

Although history and current events have preoccupied many interpreters of end-time prophecy; there have been no historical or current events connected to end time prophecy since the Day of Pentecost after the ascension of Jesus Christ. Again, there will be disagreement with that statement because of misunderstood things to come described by Jesus as recorded in Matthew 24. However, today's current events are tomorrow's history that is part of the culmination of prophecy.

YaHavah's Bible is the Judean/Christian Bible containing 66 books written over a period of time (1,806 years) from Israel's Wilderness Journey (AM 2669-AM 2709), during which time Moses recorded the first five books; to about sixty years after the crucifixion of Jesus Christ (AM 4415), when John recorded the Revelation of Jesus Christ.

The trustworthiness of the Judean/Christian Bible has been attacked from its beginning. YouTube has a plethora of videos on the untrustworthiness of the Bible thanks to atheists and secularists. Some have even attempted to rewrite the Bible to correct imagined errors.

According to the Quran's teachings, the Quran came directly to Muhammad (AD 570-AD 632), from the angel

Gabriel (Ar. *Jibril*), who received it from Almighty God (*Allah*) and then he recited it to Muhammad, piece by piece, sentence by sentence, revealing small and large portions of it over a period of 23 years. It is said that it was during a time of prayer that Gabriel came to Muhammad. Muhammad is said to have been unable to read or write, so he committed what the angel taught to memory and conveyed it to others by *recitation*. Quran means *recitation*. The Quran was not put into written form until after his death. Muhammad had a phenomenal memory. (Researched at Islamnewsroom.com and ISHK.com)

Muhammad lived in a time of a pantheon of gods and belief systems. There are always a few who believe in one God, and it appears he was one of them. In Arabic, the one God is called *Allah*.

Another "prophet" with a phenomenal memory was Joseph Smith, the founder of the Jesus Christ Latter-Day-Saints, aka, Mormonism, so named for the *Book of Mormon*. Smith claimed he was guided by an angel to a buried stash of gold tablets containing God's writings in another language. He was supposedly the only person given the ability to translate the tablets. His perspective of Bible times includes the lives and genealogy of a historically unknown people who, in 3,500 years left no archeological mark of their existence, and who are said to have had a visitation from Jesus almost immediately after he ascended to heaven. It is at this point that the New Testament is somewhat altered to accommodate this race of people who left no mark of their existence. Jesus' visitation to them was never prophesied by YaHavah as a witness of its truth.

False prophets form their own perspective of the Bible in ways that break the thread of salvation through Jesus from beginning to end causing the Bible's record of the first and second coming of Jesus Christ to be altered. The Bible tells us that the testimony of Jesus Christ is the spirit of prophecy; so, it is understandable that breaking that delicate thread would be Satan's prime target. Satan has succeeded in his mission by instilling false Bible understanding into the minds of men who are not listening to the true Spirit of YaHavah. They are not anointed by the Spirit of YaHavah.

A little clarification is needed here concerning the Greek epithet, *Christos* (Christ). Christ means, *anointed in the Spirit of YaHavah*. Jesus Christ means, *Jesus, the anointed one.* The OT Hebrew name, *Immanuel* and the epithet, *Messiah*, both mean the same as the Greek *Christ*. Those who believe in Jesus Christ are called *Christian*, which can be defined in three ways meaning the same thing. (1) O*ne who is anointed in the Spirit of YaHavah through Jesus*, (2) *YaHavah with us* (by his omnipresent Spirit), and (3) *the anointed ones* (in his omnipresent Spirit). The anointing is YaHavah with us. For the sake of familiarity, Bible translators wrote: "God with us." I use YHVH because that is how it appears in Hebrew and is specific to our Creator's person.

Jeremiah 23:23-24 *23–[Am] I Elohim at hand, said YHVH, and not Elohim afar off? 24–Can any hide himself in secret places that I shall not see him?–Said YHVH. Do I not fill heaven and earth?–Said YHVH.*

Everything we need to know is in the Judeo/Christian Bible and taught to true believers by the Spirit of YaHavah in the same way YaHavah taught his son, Jesus Christ. That means the Hebrew Old Testament and the New Testament of Jesus Christ. Everything else we learn about our world and experience from it is extra—sometimes good and sometimes bad. 1—WHAT IS A BIBLE LINEAR CALENDAR?

In 2012 the Mayan calendar had everyone's attention. No one seemed to know or care if our Creator had a calendar. Well, he does. This little booklet gathers the chronological order of people and events in Jesus's genealogy from Adam to the Babylonian captivity of Jerusalem (Judah), then moves into Daniel's seventy sevens calendar to the end.

You might wonder what a linear calendar has to do with answering the many perplexing questions we all have about the mysteries of Bible prophecy that sends the mind reeling. Which calendar is the right one? What should I believe? Which doctrine interpretation is the truth? Who can I trust to answer these questions? Where does one begin to dig out of this hole of questions? Who and what can be trusted?

The real problem is in discerning the trustworthy from the untrustworthy. There are trustworthy answers, and YaHavah provided a linear calendar that helps in the process of disabling the untrustworthy.

In accordance with Acts 17:26, the purpose of this booklet is to bring to the forefront the linear chronology of people and events leading to the fulfillment of end time prophecy, thus establishing Bible time and prophecy parameters to aid in the avoidance of false teaching.

Chronology of the Bible is a condensed view of how the righteous line was preserved for the first coming of Jesus Christ, even though all manner of opposition tried to prevent it. Even more so, today the same evil forces are trying to annihilate humanity, altogether.

AdobeStock_9660242

Every book I write addresses choices. We are pulled asunder every moment of every day with choices between good and evil. These choices began in heaven when one-third of the angels fell; choices were defined as good and evil in the Garden of Eden, Adam spread his bad choice to all his descendants. Their bad choices caused their destruction in the Great Flood; again bad choices caused the destruction of the cities of Sodom and Gomorrah, bad choices are still happening.

So, I ask, *who are you listening too?* The image here is not just a silly cartoon; it is an image of reality in the form of a cartoon because we can't normally see what angels and devils look like.

From the day, I became born again in 1980; I have searched the Bible and prayed to YaHavah for his understanding, as have many others. I have written notes, books, papers, and drew pictures of what the Bible has taught me because it helps me to understand it better, as have many others. Unlike many others, my latest effort toward a deeper understanding of prophecy led me to develop the Bible's linear calendar from Adam all the way to the end and Jubilee in New Jerusalem.

There are numerous Bible chronologies, but none like this one.

The guidelines for developing a linear calendar from the Bible are selective, in that it does not list every person and event, as do many chronological calendars. This linear calendar is comprised of Jesus' genealogy through his mother, Mary, and other people applicable in the fulfillment of prophetic events along the road to New Jerusalem.

Most of the people and events in the Bible and the world are as scenery along the roadway necessary only for historical record. The entire human race is part of the scenery, even so, not all have allowed history— past, present, and future— to distract them from the focus of the road; they are those who will not miss the call of resurrection when Jesus Christ returns. Many are called to be part of the resurrection gathering when Jesus returns, but few are chosen, because as Jesus will say of them, "I do not know you." In other words, they have broken the thread of salvation by their own choices.

YaHavah provided a Bible linear calendar in Daniel's prophecy of seventy-sevens to help us get to our destination. The prophecy of seventy-sevens contains specific signposts or parameters to keep one from straying off the road and getting lost in historical scenery along the way.

In the process of developing this calendar, I discovered a mistake I made years ago. I read a commentary that suggested the seventy-sevens started with the building and dedication of Jerusalem's wall in 444 BC. I trusted it because I was not as bold in testing doctrine as I am today. I was wrong. The seventy sevens began with Cyrus's decree for the captives to return to rebuild the temple in 528 BC or AM 3932. This is proof to me that the Bible linear calendar does help for a better understanding of difficult Scriptures because it pinpoints certain people and events. I am happy for the opportunity to humbly acknowledge and correct my mistakes publicly. Perhaps this little booklet will help others to see the Bible more clearly and humbly correct their mistakes, as well. At least, I hope that will be the result.

We all make mistakes; however, not all are willing to admit them and make corrections. For some, correction comes with a very high price. It is well to remember that nothing is more valuable than spending eternity with Jesus and YaHavah. It is the responsibility of every Christian to maintain the integrity of the thread of salvation.

Rabbinic Calculations

According to Rabbinic tradition, Messiah will come to usher in the millennial age 6000 years from the fall of Adam. Jews count the 6000 years as 2000 from the fall of Adam to Abraham, 2000 from Abraham to Messiah and 2000 years from Messiah to his return. Then 1000 years to Judgment.

Calculating a Hebrew year from a Gregorian year:

- 2055 minus 1240 plus 5000 equals 5815 / 5815 is the Hebrew year for the Gregorian year of 2055

- 2048 minus 1240 plus 5000 equals 5808 / 5808 is the Hebrew year for the Gregorian year of 2048

- 2010 minus 1240 plus 5000 equals 5770 / 5770 is the Hebrew year for the Gregorian year of 2010

It seems the Rabbi's depend on a lot of numbers and mathematical calculations. There is also a good bit of timing disagreement among Rabbinic groups. Also, they do not use Daniel's seventy sevens. With or without dates, Daniel's prophecy is the official end time calendar of years given by YaHavah to Daniel. (Dan. 9:24-27) Days, weeks, and months can be monitored by other means.

The linear calendar developed in this book makes Messianic connections for an even and clear flow of years from beginning to end. I use tables for brevity in what can be long and near boring in the telling. This booklet has proven its value to me many times as a quick reference in the process of testing doctrine and reading other end-time prophecy commentaries.

I invite you to travel with me on a quick trip through time from Eden to New Jerusalem.

2—FROM ADAM TO JACOB

The following tables show the subject focus of the various groups of years. Up to the time of Jacob, years are based on the age of the father at the birth of a son.

BEGIN COUNTING			*Years from Adam*
Father to Son	Age	AM	Reference
YHVH created Adam			Gen. 1:26
Adam to Seth	130	0-130	Gen. 5:3
Seth to Enos	105	130-235	Gen. 5:6
Enos to Cainan	90	236-325	Gen. 5:9
Cainan to Mahalaleel	70	326-395	Gen. 5:12
Mahalaleel to Jared	65	396-460	Gen. 5:15
Jared to Enoch	162	461-622	Gen. 5:18
Enoch to Methuselah	65	623-687	Gen. 5:21
Methuselah to Lamech	187	688-874	Gen. 5:25
Lamech to Noah	182	875-1056	Gen. 5:28	Noah lived 950 years to AM 2006/7
Noah to Shem, Ham, & Japheth	500	1056-1557	Gen. 5:32

For notes concerning the reason for the Great Flood, refer to Genesis Chapters Four and Six of the Word of YHVH Bible.

In the Book of Jasher Chapter 9, it tells of Abram living with Noah. Side notes in the affected tables confirm the possibility of this occurring and the accuracy of the AM timing within the tables.

Jasher Chapter 9—When Ten Years Old, Abram went to Noah and Shem, remained with them for thirty-nine years and is taught in all the ways of the Lord.

In the wickedness of Nimrod, his people purpose to build a tower to heaven to dethrone God. Then God causes confusion of tongues.

(From http://www.ccel.org/a/anonymous/jasher/home.html.)

The Ark and the Flood

THE ARK AND THE FLOOD				
Noah built the Ark and gathered creatures	100	1557-1656	Gen. 7:1 through Gen. 8:22	
Flood	1	1656-1657		Noah lived 350 years after the flood to AM 2006/7

The count continues with two post-flood years instead of Shem's age at the birth of his son because Shem was born 100 years before the flood. Those 100 years are accounted for in the flood table.

NOAH'S SON SHEM TO JACOB			
Father to Son	Age	AM	Reference
Shem to Arphaxad	2	1657-1659	Gen. 11:10
Arphaxad to Salah	35	1659-1694	Gen. 11:12
Salah to Eber	30	1694-1724	Gen. 11:14
Eber to Peleg	34	1724-1758	Gen. 11:16
Peleg to Reu	30	1758-1788	Gen. 11:18
Reu to Serug	32	1788-1820	Gen. 11:20
Serug to Nahor	30	1820-1850	Gen. 11:22
Nahor to Terah	29	1850-1879	Gen. 11:24
Terah to Abram	70	1879-1949	Gen. 11:26
Abram to Isaac	100	1949-2049	Gen. 21:5
Isaac to Jacob	60	2049-2109	Gen. 25:26
Jacob (Israel) migrates to Egypt	130	2109-2239	Gen 47:9

3—FROM EGYPT THROUGH ISRAEL's JUDGES

The tribes of Israel migrated to Egypt because of a seven-year famine prophesied by a dream had by Joseph, Jacob's eleventh son. Jacob was 130 years of age when he moved his family to Egypt. Exodus 12:40, 41 states that the time in Egypt was 430 years.

For those who compare this linear calendar with the Masoretic or Jewish chronology, you will find a large difference in years. The Jewish chronology uses 1Kings 6:1, which states that from the Exodus to the 4th year of Solomon was 480 years, but the Jewish chronology lost some of the years in Egypt, too. For whatever reason Solomon used this number, which could be a Masoretic reference to twelve generations, even so, it does not allow for 653 years of the judges from Joshua to the last period of oppression after Eli.

The counting subject is now on specific events and their length in years.

EGYPT AND THE WILDERNESS JOURNEY			
Name	Yrs.	AM	Ref.
In Egypt	430	2239-2669	Genesis 15:13; Exodus 12:40, 41
In the Wilderness	40	2669-2709	Exodus 14:27-31

Israel's judges are the next linear subject. Note how many times the people were overtaken by oppressors and turned back to Baal worship.

Before we move on to the table for the Judges, a point of possible interest is in the Book of Joshua. Joshua 1:13 mentions a prophecy in the Book of Jasher concerning the day the sun stood still for Joshua.

Joshua orders the sun and moon to stand still.

Joshua 10:12-15 *"12—Then spoke Joshua to YHVH in the day when YHVH delivered up the Amorites before the children of Israel, and he said in the sight of Israel, Sun, stand you still upon Gibeon; and you, Moon, in the valley of Ajalon. 13—And the sun stood still, and the moon stayed, until the people had avenged themselves upon their enemies. [Is] not this written in the book of Jasher? So the sun stood still in the midst of heaven and hasted not to go down about a whole day. 14—And there was no day like that before it or after it, that YHVH hearkened to the voice of a man: for YHVH fought for Israel. 15—And Joshua returned, and all Israel with him, to the camp to Gilgal."*

Joshua 10:12-13—Question: Can the event that took place in Joshua 10:13 be confirmed, for example by counting the positions of heavenly bodies backward in time?

"In general, trying to prove events that are said to have occurred in the Bible, using scientific principles, doesn't work. Most scientists draw a clear distinction between things that are taken on faith and those that are testable and therefore falsifiable. Science deals with the latter, and religion with the former."

Quoted from Ask an Astrophysicist at the website for NASA Goddard Space Flight Center, http://imagine.gsfc.nasa.gov/ask_astro/earth.html Question ID: 980902d Can science confirm the missing

17

day referred to in the Bible? (Submitted March 25, 1997)

According to the full article, NASA has never officially, or unofficially, conducted any tests to prove or disprove that the sun stood still for any length of time at any point in the past. Does this mean it did not happen? No. However, the Book of Jasher or The Upright is an apocryphal book. Keep in mind that the earth revolves around the sun, while the sun holds a steady place in space. The earth would have to stop revolving in order for the sun to appear in one place for any length of time; if that happened, it would cause displacement of the stars. The changes that would occur in the appearance of the heavens is inestimable by the mind of man or any computer.

Joshua's quote from the Book of Jasher is more likely a metaphor for what appeared to be an impossible battle won in one day at the hand of YHVH. The point of Joshua 10:12-13 is that Joshua's heart was for YHVH. He trusted that YHVH would be in battle with him. That is the why and how of a battle won. As phenomenal as signs and wonders are, it is far better to know that YHVH stands with those whose hearts are for him. (Quoted from the Word of YHVH Bible Notes for Joshua 10:12-13.)

The Book of Joshua does not clearly state how many years Joshua judged, however, it does say he became judge at age 40, and he died at age 110. Joshua judged Israel 70 years. The years for the following table are based on the years of service as judge.

The Bible does not clearly state how many years there was rebellion toward YaHavah after Samson died. The Bible does tell us that Eli judged 40 years and died at age 98. That leaves 58 years of oppression between Eli and Samson.

JUDGES IN THE PROMISED LAND Years are based on years of service as judge				
Name	Yrs.	AM	Note	Ref.
Joshua	70	2709-2779		Joshua 1:1-4; Judges 2:8
Generation of Baal	40	2779-2819	Oppressors	Judges 2:10-17
Othniel	40	2819-2859		Judges 3:9-11
Eglon	18	2859-2877	Oppressors	Judges 3:12-14
Ehud	80	2877-2957		Judges 3:15-29
Shamgar	1	2957-2958		Judges 3:31
Jabin	20	2958-2978	Oppressors	Judges 4:1-3
Deborah	40	2978-3018		Judges 4:4 through 5:31
Midian	7	3018-3025	Oppressors	Judges 6:1
Gideon	40	3025-3065		Judges 6:11-- 8:32
Abimelech	3	3065-3068		Judges 9:22-55
Tola	23	3068-3091		Judges 10:1-2

Jair	22	3091-3113		Judges 10:1-5
Philistines	40	3113-3153	Oppressors	Judges 10:6-17
Jephthah	6	3153-3159		Judges 11:18--12:7
Ibzan	7	2159-3166		Judges 12:8-9
Elon	10	3166-3176		Judges 12:11-12
Abdon	8	3176-3184		Judges 12:13-15
Philistines	40	3184-3224	Oppressors	Judges 13:1
Samson	20	3224-3244		Judges 13:2--16:31
The people turned from YHVH	58	3244-3302	Oppressors	Judges 21:25
Eli	40	3302-3342		1Samuel 4:15-18
Philistines stole the ark of the covenant	20	3342-3362	Oppressors	1Samuel 4:12-17; 7:2

4—ISRAEL'S UNITED AND SPLIT KINGDOMS

Now the linear count subject turns to the kings of the twelve tribes of Israel (Jacob). Paul stated in Acts 13:20 that the people were under Judges for about 450 years. Count 40 years under Moses and 410 years of judges to equal 450 years. The actual time from Egypt to Samuel is 693 years, leaving 243 years under oppressors. It seems they didn't want to claim the bad years, even though they did happen.

They cried out to YaHavah for a king when they grew weary under their oppressors.

The United Kingdom

King	Yrs.	AM	Reference
Saul	40	3362-3402	Acts 13:21
David	40	3402-3442	2Samuel 5:4
Solomon	40	3442-3482	1Kings 11:42

The Book of Acts is the only reference to the actual length of Saul's reign.

Timing Problems Encountered

Except for the first kings of the split kingdom, the remaining kings started their reign in a specified year of a former king, either of the North in Samaria, or South in Jerusalem. The references bounce back and forth but are amazingly accurate. The number of years I used are rounded but do balance in the overall time.

21

Names have a history of repeating in families. The Bible is no different. In the following table, Ahab, the king of Israel in the North, had sons named Ahaziah and Joram, aka, Jehoram. Jehoshaphat had a son named Jehoram and Jehoram had a son named Ahaziah; so that, both, the kingdom of Israel and the kingdom of Judah, had kings of the same name within the same period of fourteen years.

Another thing to watch for in the Bible is conflicting times. Such is the case in the reign of Joram, son of Ahab. Also, one reference states Ahab had no son, while another reference names Joram as his son, perhaps because he reigned in his stead.

2Kings 1:17—*"so he [Ahab] died according to the word of YHVH which Elijah had spoken. And Joram reigned in his stead in the second year of Jehoram the son of Jehoshaphat king of Judah; because he had no son."*

2Kings 3:1—*Now, Jehoram [Joram] the son of Ahab began to reign over Israel in Samaria the eighteenth year of Jehoshaphat king of Judah, and reigned twelve years.*

The scribe or translator apparently made an error. The decision on whether to use the reference of the 18th year of Jehoshaphat or the 2nd year of Jehoram the son of Jehoshaphat was determined for me by the fact that Jehoram must use Joram to determine the year of his reign. We must first use the 18th year of Jehoshaphat to determine the time of Joram, the son of Ahab.

Overlapping linear years in the record of the split kingdoms can appear to be contradictory; however, the linear calendar can clear that up, too. Up to the record of the split kingdoms, the total years equaled the linear dates. In the kingdom of Israel, some kings served at the same time or seriously overlapped in time. For instance, Jotham, king of the North, reigned sixteen years within the twenty years of

Pekah, king of the North. The Northern kingdom sometimes had differing kings at the same time. Even so, the Bible uses both, Israel and Judah, to calculate the total. The linear calendar follows the years for the kings of Judah or the Southern Kingdom. The years of the Northern Kingdom are like a check system to arrive at the right dates for the Southern Kingdom without neglecting the ten tribes in Samaria.

The linear years of the Northern and Southern kingdoms are solely for calculating the beginning of the end-time prophecy of Daniel's Seventy-sevens. Remember, the Bible linear calendar is for understanding the road signs (prophecies) on the path to Jesus' return.

The Split Kingdom

Kings	Judah	Israel	AM	Note	Reference
Rehoboam	17		3482-3499		1Kings 11:42; 14:21
Jeroboam I		22	3482-3504		1Kings 11:19
Abijah	3		3500-3503	18th year of Jeroboam	1Kings 15:1
Asa	41		3502-3543	20th year of Jeroboam	1Kings 15:9
Nadab		2	3504-3506	2nd year of Asa	1Kings 15:25
Baasha		24	3505-3529	3rd year of Asa	1Kings 15:33

Elah		2	3528-3530	26th year of Asa	1Kings 16:1
Zimri —7 days			3529	27th year of Asa	1Kings 16:15
Tibni		5	3529-3534		1Kings 16:21-22
Omri		12	3533-3545	31st year of Asa	1Kings 16:23
Ahab		22	3540-3562	38th year of Asa	1Kings 16:29
Jehoshaphat	25		3544-3569	4th year of Ahab	1Kings 22:41
Ahaziah — son of Ahab		2	3561-3563	17th year of Jehoshaphat	1Kings 22:40, 51
Joram (Jehoram), son of Ahab		12	3562-3574	18th year of Jehoshaphat	2Kings 1:17; 2Kings 3:1
Jehoram, son of Jehoshaphat	8		3567-3575	5th year of Joram	1Kings 22:50; 2Kings 8:16
Ahaziah, son of Jehoram	1		3574-3575	12th year of Joram	2kings 8:25
Jehu-son of Jehoshaphat		28	3575-3603	Anointed by priest to be king of Israel	2Kings 9:1-10

24

Athaliah, (Queen)	6		3575-3582	She killed all potential heirs to the throne except Joash, who was hidden	2Kings 11:1-2
Joash	40		3582-3622	7th year of Jehu	2Kings 12:1
Jehoahaz		17	3605-3622	23rd year of Joash	2Kings 13:1
Jehoash		16	3619-3635	37th year of Joash	2Kings 13:10
Amaziah	29		3621-3650	2nd year of Jehoash	2Kings 14:1
Jeroboam II		41	3635-3676	15th year of Amaziah	2Kings 13:8-10, 14:15-16,23
Uzziah, (Azariah)	52		3662-3714	27th year of Jeroboam II	2Kings 15:1
Zachariah	6 mo.		3700	38th year of Uzziah	2Kings 15:8
Shallum	1 mo.		3701	39th year of Uzziah	2Kings 15:13
Menahem		10	3701-3711	39th year of Uzziah	2Kings 15:17
Pehahiah		2	3712-3714	50th year of Uzziah	2Kings 15:23

Pekah		20	3714-3734	52nd year of Uzziah	2Kings 15:27
Jotham	16		3716-3731	2nd year of Pekah	2Kings 15:32
Ahaz	16		3731-3747	17th year of Pekah	2Kings 16:1
Hoshea		9	3743-3752	12th year of Ahaz	2Kings 17:1
Samaria fell to Assyria			3752 AM	723 BC—accepted year	2Kings 17:6

The Northern Kingdom of Israel in Samaria fell to Assyria in AM 3752. The generally accepted historical date is 723 BC—2Kings 17:6

The Northern Kingdom fell, and the Southern Kingdom continued.

The Southern Kingdom of Judah

Kings of Judah	Yrs.	AM	Note	Reference
Hezekiah	29	3746-3775	3rd year of Hoshea (Hezekiah)	2Kings 18:1
Manasseh	55	3775-3830	succeeded Hezekiah	2Kings 21:1
Amon	2	3830-3832	succeeded Manasseh	2Kings 21:19
Josiah	31	3832-	succeeded	2Kings 22:1

		3863	Amon	
Jehoahaz	3 mo.	3863	succeeded Josiah	2Kings 23:31
Jehoiakim	11	3863-3874	succeeded Jehoahaz	2Kings 23:34
Jehoiachin	3 mo.	3874	succeeded Jehoiakim	2Kings 24:6-8
Zedekiah	11	3874-3885	appointed by the king of Babylon	2Kings 24:18
Jerusalem fell to Babylon		3885 AM	The generally accepted historical date is 584 BC	2Kings 25:1-8

The Southern Kingdom of Judah at Jerusalem fell to Babylon in AM 3885. The generally accepted historical date is 584 BC (2Kings 25:1-8)

A Synopsis of the Fall of Jerusalem

Josiah went up against Necho, the king of Egypt who was fighting against Carchemish by the Euphrates. Necho questioned why Josiah was coming against him because Elohim had told Necho not to fight Josiah. Josiah disguised himself, fought with Necho's army, and met his death. (2Chronicles 35:20-27)

Jehoahaz reigned three months until Necho took him to Egypt. (2Chronicles 36:1-3) The king of Egypt put Jehoiakim, the brother of Jehoahaz, on the throne. Daniel reports that in the third year of Jehoiakim, Nebuchadnezzar besieged Jerusalem and took some of the sons of Israel, including some of the royal family, nobles, and perfect youths showing intelligence from every branch of wisdom. Daniel was among them. (Daniel 1:1-4)

Jehoiakim reigned eleven years until Nebuchadnezzar of Babylon took him to Babylon. (2Chronicles 36:4-8) This marked the beginning of Nebuchadnezzar's power over Israel, (605-562 BC), but the prophesied destruction of Jerusalem would not come for nearly twenty years.

Jehoiachin succeeded to the throne and reigned three months when Nebuchadnezzar took him to Babylon. (2Chronicles 36:9-10) The king of Babylon took all the fighting men, artisans, and wise men to Babylon, but Jerusalem had still not fallen completely to Babylon.

Zedekiah was on the throne for nine years, when he attempted to go against Nebuchadnezzar and failed. Nebuchadnezzar then encamped around Jerusalem for two years. In the eleventh year of Zedekiah, Nebuchadnezzar took the city and burned the temple. (2Chronicles 36:11-19)

YaHavah Elohim sent prophets Jeremiah and Habakkuk to turn Zedekiah back to YaHavah, but the people would not listen. The consequence was that Elohim sent Nebuchadnezzar against Jerusalem to destroy the city. (Jeremiah 50:1 through 52:34)

Please understand that we are all in the midst of a spiritual war that started in heaven before creation. Realized or not, it is raging every moment resulting in catastrophe and desolation in many areas and lives on this earth.

Throughout the entire time of the kings, YaHavah gave the people prophets to warn them that if they did not turn back to him, they would suffer the consequences. All of the kings of the Northern Kingdom in Samaria were evil, so they suffered the consequences of their choice. Assyria captured them and dispersed them. The ten tribes of Israel and the two tribes of Judah will reunite in the Spirit of YaHavah on the day their currently rejected Messiah, Jesus Christ, returns.

The twelve tribes have been divided for 2,500 years because they chose to do it their way. What makes "Christians" think their denominational divisions will be excused by YaHavah? Into what are they baptized? Certainly, not in the unity of the Spirit of YaHavah.

Half of the kings of Judah, or the Southern Kingdom were evil, which is why Jesus' genealogy to Mary, his mother, came through David's son Nathan, not Solomon.

Are we there yet? Where is the calendar?

Not quite, but we are still on the road of prophecy leading to Jesus Christ and his return. The calendar will be revealed in due time.

The captivity recap table below shows the number of years of Judah's captivity from the temple's destruction, which is seventy years. During the seventy years, the temple began to be restored, and the timing of Daniel's seventy sevens began. Many years later, the wall of Jerusalem was restored.

CAPTIVITY RECAP			
Total captivity years	70	3885-3955 AM	Ezra 6:15
Start Seventy-sevens		3932 AM	Daniel 9:25 (537 BC)

After Daniel's seventy-sevens of years started, other prophecies had to be fulfilled for the background of future signpost prophecies. So, before we go to the Sabbath linear calendar, we will discuss the first two beasts of Daniel's visions of four beasts.

5—FIRST TWO BEASTS OF DANIEL

Too many cooks ruin the stew, and that is what happened to the order of Daniel's writings. His time as YaHavah's prophet covered a span of 83 years from AM 3866 to 3949. Those whose hands his writings fell into could not understand any of it. As a result, the prophecies were shuffled into general disorder. The book was labeled as Jewish fable until it was canonized into the Judeo/Christian Bible. When the writings were set into chapters, they remained out of the order in which they were written. The Word of YHVH Bible set them in the order of the years of the kings Daniel noted. (Chapter numbering is explained in the WYB introduction to Danial.)

After the fall of Jerusalem, the linear year subject turns to the kings of Babylon and the captivity of Jerusalem, which introduces the first three beasts of Daniel's prophecy of four great beasts. The next linear change is centered on Daniel's prophecy of the four beasts, but specifically, the first two.

The number of years Nebuchadnezzar ruled over Babylon is history. For this calendar, we are only interested in the number of years he ruled over the captivity of Jerusalem.

FIRST BEAST OF DANIEL, ONE KING			
Kings over Babylon	Yrs.	AM	Reference
Nebuchadnezzar, First Beast—Lion	24	3885-3909	Jeremiah 25:1-3 (585 BC)
Other kings of Babylon	23	3909-3932	

Second Beast of Daniel

The second beast consisted of three kings who were Persian and Mede. The first king, Cyrus the Persian, wrote a decree authorizing the restoration of the temple at Jerusalem. Cambyses II, aka, Ahasuerus reigned seven years (AM 3942-3949) between Cyrus and Darius. Babylonians during the reign of Cambyses II opposed rebuilding the temple and caused work to cease. Even though Cambyses is not part of the second beast, he did play a part in preventing the annihilation of the captives while the work on the temple was at a halt—see the Book of Esther and Daniel 9:1.

SECOND BEAST OF DANIEL—THREE KINGS			
Kings over Babylon	Yrs.	AM	Reference/notes
1 Cyrus writes a decree to rebuild the temple	10	3932-3942	Daniel 9:24-25; Isaiah 44:24-28 (528 BC)
- Cambyses II aka, Ahasuerus	7	3942-3949	Book of Esther and Daniel 9:1, (not part of the second beast)
2 Darius I honors the decree to finish the temple	6	3949-3955	Ezra 6:1, (temple completed in 515 BC)
- Darius I stopped the opposition against the temple. The temple was completed in 515 BC			
- One king reigned over Babylon	21	3955-3976	Between Darius I and Artaxerxes, I Longimanus

3	Artaxerxes I Longimanus, grandson of Darius	41	3976-4017	Artaxerxes I issued a decree in his 20th year to rebuild the wall of Jerusalem, correlating with Daniel 9:25. Nehemiah 2:1; 6:15; 8:1-18 (445 BC)

Building the Wall of Jerusalem

Nehemiah left Babylon in the 1st month (Nisan) of AM 3996 (445 BC) and arrived in Jerusalem in the 4th month (Tammuz). The wall was finished in 52 days in the 6th month (Elul). In the seventh month (Tishri), AM 3996 (445 BC), Nehemiah read the Law and the congregation celebrated the Feast of Ingathering. (Nehemiah 2:1; 6:15; 8:1-18) This completed the acts of the first two beasts known as the lion and the bear.

Daniel prophesied about four beasts. We will discuss the correlation of the last two described as a leopard and a dragon later. But first, we will begin the seventy-sevens timing I call YaHavah's end time calendar. The last two beasts come within the timing of this calendar.

6—BEGIN THE SEVENTY-SEVENS OF DANIEL

The Last Change in Counting Linear Years

The seventy-sevens are based on Sabbath, which means rest. Bible Sabbaths are the seventh day for people, seventh year for land, and the fiftieth year for Jubilee Sabbath, also being land and people Sabbath. (Leviticus 25:1-22)

The next section is the Sabbath linear calendar beginning in the first year of Cyrus, AM 3932 (539 BC) and continuing to the end and New Jerusalem. From the beginning of the seventy-sevens calendar to the birth of Christ is 450 years. Interesting that this is the same number of years for the judges of Israel.

Sabbath Linear to the End

The Book of Daniel is critical to the understanding of end-time prophecy and of when the end-times begin and end. This is where many Bible interpreters have left the road to stumble in the forest. It seems there are as many interpretations as there are interpreters. And even they refuse to define their interpretations with certainty. They usually rely on citations from other expositors then agree or disagree without any real explanation of why. However, the Bible says there is only one interpretation, and that is the one we want to find within the Scriptures.

Daniels' seventy-sevens provide a Sabbath format to create the Sabbath linear calendar. This is the beginning of the right road to New Jerusalem. I call it Route 77, and this is what makes this book and calendar unique.

Daniel 9:24—[24]—Seventy weeks are determined upon your people and upon your holy city, to finish the transgression, and to make an end of sins, and to make reconciliation for iniquity, and to bring in

33

everlasting righteousness, and to seal up the vision and prophecy, and to anoint the most Holy.

Daniel 9:25-26a —*25—Know therefore and understand, [that]* **after the going forth of the commandment to restore and to build Jerusalem to the Messiah the Prince [shall be] seven weeks,** *and threescore and two weeks: the street shall be built again, and the wall, even in troublous times. 26a—And after threescore and two weeks shall Messiah be cut off, but not for himself.*

Daniel 9:26b-27 *26b—The people of the prince that shall come shall batter and corrupt the city and the sanctuary; and the end thereof [shall be] with a flood, and to the end of the war desolations are determined. 27—And he shall confirm the covenant with many for one week: and in the midst of the week he shall cause the sacrifice and the tribute to cease, and because of the overspreading of abominations he shall make [it] waste, even to the end, and that decreed shall be poured upon the ruined.*

According to Daniel 9:25, the seventy weeks begin with Cyrus' decree to restore Jerusalem and the temple. There are no other linear calendar changes from this point forward. The Sabbath linear timing will remain to the end counted in 49-year blocks of seven Land Sabbaths. I prefer to call them Jubilee blocks in anticipation of the eternal Jubilee with our Lord and Savior.

The remnant of Israel is the primary people in this prophecy. YaHavah promised he would redeem a remnant of the twelve tribes, who at the time of the return of their Messiah will be rejoined. There are many Bible references to the remnant; however, the best is in the Song of Solomon which describes the remnant of Israel as the sleeping bride. The Book of Revelation sets the number of the remnant of Israel at 144,000 souls. Keep in mind that it is a last-minute deliverance of the remnant before the Son of Man (Jesus) is seen descending on a cloud from heaven. From the cross up to that moment, every living soul, both Jew and Gentile, had, has, or will have the opportunity to accept their Messiah, Jesus Christ, to lead them into the kingdom of YaHavah.

I keep hearing a resounding question concerning the salvation of the aborigine, Indians, Eskimo, and all the people who were and now are not connected to channels of communication to hear the truth of Jesus Christ. That is like asking how many angels can dance on the head of a pin. No one can answer either question. Neither does anyone know what is in the mind of YaHavah except for that which we have in the Judeo/Christian Bible. All doctrine and questions must be measured by what we have in the Bible. There is no other Bible that has the truth of Jesus Christ and what we are to do until he returns. We cannot do anything about the past, but we can reach as many souls today and tomorrow as each of us is able.

In the Song of Solomon, the Bride's companions are the daughters of Jerusalem, described elsewhere as other people or Gentiles who are faithful to YaHavah. There are differing notions as to the meaning of the Song. Assuming that the Song is for a future time, we may also assume the daughters of Jerusalem are the Saints of Jesus Christ, aka, Christians and sisters of the Bride. This is in accordance with what the Bible teaches. Rest assured, that the Christian Church has not taken the place of the Bride. That belongs to the remnant of Israel. However, when Jesus returns to gather his bride, he will also gather the faithful saints who cared for his Bride in his absence. They will be the last to receive the Spirit seal, and they will rise together with all the Saints.

Her companions are instructed not to awaken his Bride before the Bridegroom returns. The Bride (a remnant of Israel) and her companions (Christians) all remain together until the Bridegroom comes to take them to the house he and his father have prepared. The word, *remain*, in this context means those who are alive at the time of the last seven years of Daniel's prophecy. Choices made and kept at the time of death are permanent and will tell at the time of resurrection when Jesus returns.

Note that the seventy sevens of weeks cannot end until Jesus returns to fulfill his millennial reign. The proof is in everlasting righteousness which Jesus will bring with him at his second coming. Only then, can there be no more sin, regardless of how many Bible scholars say sin was finished at the cross of Christ or at any other perceived time. The cross offers reconciliation to those who will accept Jesus Christ as Lord and Savior. Even so, we have only to look at all the wars and other abominations toward YaHavah to see that everlasting righteousness is not yet here.

Note, too, that none of Daniel's prophecies include any **secret** calling out for the Saints before, in the middle, or at the end of the last seven years as it is understood in many false teachings. The operative word is **secret**. As a matter of fact, the only secrets are the ones Satan has inspired.

Jerusalem was released from the physical kingdom of Babylon only to step into a world filled with the spirit of Babylon the Bible calls the *Mother of Harlots*. This Babylonian captivity will remain in the world for all who reject the truth of Jesus until Jesus returns.

The last seven years is the final sifting of all ethnic groups and people of all religious beliefs, including the then living Christians, which means the entire world population who are alive when the last seven years begins.

SEVENTY LAND SABBATHS OR 490 YEARS, PLUS				
Event	Yrs.	AM	Note:	Reference:
7 Land Sabbaths	49	3932-3980	Sabbath pattern	Daniel 9:25
To the birth of Jesus	401	3980-4381	57 Land Sabbaths plus 2 years	Matthew 1:18-25; Luke 1:26-28
To the baptism and anointing of Jesus	30	4381-4412	Baptism of Jesus	Isaiah 11:1-2; Matthew 3:16
To 62 Land Sabbaths	3	3981-4414	Crucifixion, resurrection, ascension	Daniel 9:24; Matthew 27:33 through 28:18; Acts 1:10
One Land Sabbath	7	To begin unknown	The seven trumpets of seal seven	Revelation Chapters 8 through 11

The total of the first two time designations 7 weeks and 62 weeks is 483 years. The third designation of 7 years will be discussed next.

7—PATTERN OF THE SEVENTY SEVENS PROPHECY

We have arrived. We can now see what the Bible's calendar or YaHavah's calendar looks like and how the Bible explains it. It is set and cannot be changed.

PATTERN OF FIRST SEVEN SEVENS						
3932	3933	3934	3935	3936	3937	3938
3939	3940	3941	3942	3943	3944	3945
3946	3947	3948	3949	3950	3951	3952
3953	3954	3955	3956	3957	3958	3959
3960	3961	3962	3963	3964	3965	3966
3967	3968	3969	3970	3971	3972	3973
3974	3975	3976	3977	3978	3979	3980

- Begin counting when Cyrus decreed to rebuild the temple in AM 3932

- Jesus birth AM 4382
- Baptized AM 4412
- End of 62 weeks
- Jesus' death, resurrection, and ascension AM 4415

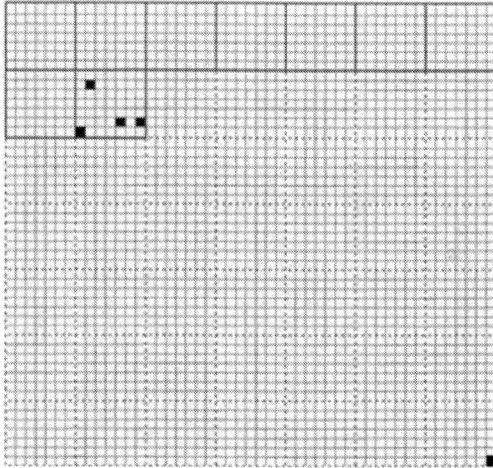

Year AM 6381 (2000 AD)

The last seven years of each succeeding block of 49 years is the potential last seven years of Daniel's seventy sevens prophecy.

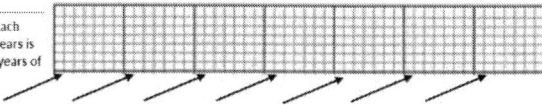

The solid bordered blocks in the image contain the first two time-periods of seven weeks (49 years) and sixty-two weeks (434 years) equaling 483 years.

There are 49 blocks in the larger main section. I chose to begin a new section of a possible set of 49 blocks to show how the calendar continues until the end. I believe the focus of Jesus' return is on the last Land Sabbath of a block of 49 years, whether it is the current block or a future block is yet to be revealed.

The large main body of blocks in the center contains 2,401 years which ended 2000 years after the birth of Christ. See the section 8—"Where are we in 2017?"

Each block contains seven Land Sabbaths or forty-nine years as prophesied in Daniel's prophecy of seventy sevens. During the seventy sevens— of which we are still in—the land will enjoy its Land Sabbaths without Israel's participation. (Leviticus 26:33-35)

The next block of time, sixty-two weeks, is in the 9th block from the pattern and contains the end of the sixty-two weeks (AM 4414). Jesus' birth was 33 years before the end of 62 weeks.

JESUS HAS HIS OWN 49-YEAR BLOCK						
4373	4374	4375	4376	4377	4378	4379
4380	4381	4382	4383	4384	4385	4386
4387	4388	4389	4390	4391	4392	4393
4394	4395	4396	4397	4398	4399	4400
4401	4402	4403	4404	4405	4406	4407
4408	4409	4410	4411	4412	4413	4414
4415	4416	4417	4418	4419	4420	4421

AM 4412 He was anointed at age 30

After 62 weeks (AM 4415)—his crucifixion, resurrection, and the release of the Spirit at Pentecost. Rev. 5:6

The next table describes the events of the above block belonging to Jesus. ascension, and glorification in heaven to pour out

AM	EVENT	Time of YHVH's Feasts
4382	birth of Christ (AD 1 or?)	Near Passover (see the introduction to the gospel of Luke in the Word of YHVH Bible)
4412	baptism of Christ (AD 30)	Near Passover
4414	end of 62 sevens (AD 33)	
4415	after 62 sevens; death, resurrection, (AD 34)	Passover
4415	ascension of Christ and promised Comforter came as the seven-spirit anointing	Pentecost
Unknown	Jesus will return	Feast of Ingathering (Jesus returns on a cloud to call his sealed saints just as he left)

Creating the calendar from the words of the Bible does not require any math or coding skills. The Spirit is the teacher and the Bible is the resource.

Jesus came to fulfill the Law and prophecy. He is the center of YaHavah's three Feasts called the Passover, Pentecost, and Ingathering.

The highpoints of his first coming and ascension were at or near the first two Feasts—**Passover and Pentecost**.

His second coming will be at the time of the **Feast of Ingathering**. At the seventh trumpet, in that Land Sabbath year, Jesus' will call from a cloud to gather his sealed saints, including the sealed remnant of Israel. There is no need for complicated timelines; YaHavah has given us his timeline in Daniel's seventy sevens prophecy.

Clarification of terms

There is need of some clarification between the terms *end-times, end-time, and last days.* The table of 49-year boxes above is a birds-eye view of the years from AM 3932-6479 or 2,548 years. Its entirety is in the scope of the *end-times (plural)* and what Jesus called *this generation.* Some historians and theologians call world generations, *dispensations.*

Last days and *end-time* (singular) are more likely to apply to the last seven years.

The Bible describes human generations and world generations.

Human creation by YHVH was accomplished in three unrepeated stages or generations. These three, produced physical and spirit-DNA (we are all sinners through Adam) that is passed on to future generations.

1. **Adam** was created from the dust of the earth and *life breathed into him by YHVH.*

2. **Eve** was created from a rib bone from Adam and *life breathed into her by YHVH.* Humans, male and female, were created for the purpose of procreation by the union of male and female and *life is breathed into their offspring by YHVH.*

3. **YHVH created Jesus** in the womb of a virgin maiden without the benefit of a human male and *life was breathed into him by his father, YHVH.* Jesus did not have a human father; therefore, Jesus was born without the sin of Adam on his soul that all other humans are born with. This is critical to understand about the necessary humanity of Jesus.

Neither his body nor his soul (spirit) existed prior to his conception and birth. We can be certain of this fact because beings created before the creation of our heavens and earth were created to be what they are, angels who are YHVH's host and his messengers. They can neither procreate nor become human at will. Only mythology claims other gods in the heavens. YaHavah is the first and the last in all eternity.

There are four broad world generations related to the sin condition of humanity:

1. Creation of the heavens and earth—entrance of sin

2. After the Great Flood—destruction of sinful humanity except for Noah and his immediate family—eight persons

3. Seventy sevens calendar from physical Babylonian captivity to the return of Jesus— *under the spiritual captivity of Babylon, the Mother of Harlots*

4. Millennial reign of Jesus on earth—complete freedom from sin while Satan is in chains

Jesus referred to "this generation" several times in his teachings, or at least it was recorded several times. His reference was to all generations of humanity within the seventy-sevens calendar or item #3.

43

The time between the beginning of the **chronological** *70th week* and the beginning of the **prophetic** *70th week* is commonly referred to as the **gap**.

Thirty years ago, I realized there is no unknown gap in the seventy-sevens prophecy. The last seven years must be connected with a continuous count of years, ergo, YaHavah's Calendar. I could see it then, but was afraid to say it. The fear of YaHavah has replaced my fear of peer recrimination. I thought it best to march to the sound of his drums to the end.

Jesus was crucified at the beginning of the *chronological 70th week,* and he will return at the end of the *prophetic 70th week.* In a sense, he is the beginning and the end of the 70th week.

The calendar continues. Please understand that this is YaHavah's calendar to the end devised and followed by him. I am quite certain he doesn't care what we think about it as long as we understand and use it the way he means for it to be used.

The land will not have each of the twelve tribes in the boundaries of their promised land until the millennium, when they may enter their land reunited and without sin. This did not happen in 1948 when many Jews migrated into Israel from other countries. The Jewish exodus into Jerusalem in 1948 is only a point of time in history and the vision of certain people who took a misunderstood prophecy into their own hands, not YaHavah's fulfillment of that prophecy.

Daniel's prophecy of seventy-sevens gives all end time prophecy its form and parameters. The last days of the seventieth seven is preparing to show itself. We have waited a long time and not very patiently; come Lord Jesus.

8—WHERE ARE WE NOW—IN 2017?

Jesus died and ascended in the 42nd year of the chronological last seven years of his 49-year block. The pattern and prophecy tell us that he will return at the beginning of the 49th year of the current or future 49-year block. The millennium is also the 49th year which is a Land Sabbath. (2Peter 3:8) All of the laws of Land Sabbath will be applied. The end of the millennium will end all prophecy and visions and begin eternal Jubilee. The total timing of Daniel's seventy sevens takes us to that great day. See 11—Chronological order of the Bible for a full recap.

Below is the *41st block of 49 years from the Cross of Christ. AD 2017 is AM 6398*. Gregorian dates are shown on the right side of the 49-year blocks below. We do not know the day or hour, but YaHavah has provided a calendar to know that the last seven years will be at the end of a forty-nine-year block because the calendar was established on Sabbath, the Three Feasts of YaHavah, and Jubilee. In the following block, the year of Jubilee will be AM 6431.

41st Block of 49-years from Jesus							AD
6382	6383	6384	6385	6386	6387	6388	2007
6389	6390	6391	6392	6393	6394	6395	2014
6396	6397	6398	6399	6400	6401	6402	2021 AM 6398 is AD 2017
6403	6404	6405	6406	6407	6408	6409	2028
6410	6411	6412	6413	6414	6415	6416	2035
6417	6418	6419	6420	6421	6422	6423	2042
6424	6425	6426	6427	6428	6429	6430	2049 (possible, not probable, last seven years of Daniel)

The Jewish chronological calendar year for Rosh Hashanah 2017, (Sept) is AM 5778. There is a 620-year difference in this calendar and the Jewish linear calendar, yet another major difference in years from the calculations of item *3—From Egypt Through Israel's Judges*. The time from the beginning of judges (Joshua) to their first king (Saul) is 653 years.

Below is the 42nd block of 49 years from the Cross of Christ. The last seven years of each new block of 49 years is potentially the last seven years before the return of Christ as previously explained. I, or anyone else, can only project calculations for the return of Christ by the clearly stated commands and timing given by YaHavah. No one knows but YaHavah; however, he has given us partial insight into his knowledge.

42nd Block of 49-years from Jesus							AD	
6431	6432	6433	6434	6435	6436	6437	2056	
6438	6439	6440	6441	6442	6443	6444	2063	
6445	6446	6447	6448	6449	6450	6451	2070	
6452	6453	6434	6455	6456	6457	6458	2077	
6459	6460	6461	6462	6463	6464	6465	2084	
6466	6467	6468	6469	6470	6471	6472	2091	
6473	6474	6475	6476	6477	6478	6479	2098	(Possible, not probable, last seven years of Daniel)

We cannot know the day or hour, but those who are alive during the last seven years will know three days before Jesus returns, because that is when the two prophets of YaHavah will be killed to lay in the streets for three days before they are resurrected.

Those who have listened to the Spirit will know they have six years of extreme tribulation ahead of them when a seven year agreement is made that culminates in a inferno of forest fires world wide. As of 2010, forests cover 31 percent of the world's land surface, just over 4 billion hectares. (One hectare = 2.47 acres.) In acres, that is 9.9 billion acres. One-third is 3.3 billion acres of trees. http://www.fao.org/forest-resources-assessment/en/

9—THE 70TH WEEK AND THE FOURTH BEAST

The last seven years of Daniel's prophecy brings in the Fourth Beast described in Daniel 8:8-27 and Revelation 13:1-18. One week, aka, seven years, or seventieth week, is yet to come. (Daniel 9:26b-27)

There are no prophecy signposts on the road after the cross of Christ until just before the last seven years begins. The *seven-year agreement of many* is the next sign and marks the starting point. Everything else between the ascension of Christ and the first year of the last seven years is the making of history and the birth pangs of the earth described by Jesus to his disciples.

The ensuing seven trumpets described in the seventh seal on the scroll with seven seals are the yearly warnings of the approaching Great Day of YaHavah along the remainder of the road. (Read the Book of Joel) All of the current pre, mid, and post tribulation theories believe the entire scroll represents the last seven years.

Seven Trumpet Warning for the Great Day of YHVH

Each year of the last seven years will be announced by the sound of a trumpet warning us that the Day of YaHavah is near. The Book of Joel corresponds to Revelation Chapters 8 through 11 describing the occurrences of the seven trumpets and Jesus' description of the days before his return.

Joel is the book of the watchman urging humankind to seek the name of YHVH and to know the signs for the coming Day of YHVH when the remnant will be sealed before the sound of the seventh trumpet and taken with the faithful saints to meet Jesus in the air. (Joel 2 and 3; Revelation 7:1-8; Revelation 8: 1 through 11:19)

Joel's trumpets of warning are the same trumpets of the seventh seal on the scroll with seven seals. The Day of YaHavah or Great Day of YaHavah is 1,000 years long and will occur during a Land Sabbath year. At the beginning of that Land Sabbath, the seven and last trumpet of warning will be sounded.

2Peter 3:8—*But, beloved, be not ignorant of this one thing, that one day [is], with our Adonai, as a thousand years, and a thousand years as one day.*

The Great Day is the seventh day of the seventieth week. In this context, day and year are synonymous. Our Lord Jesus Christ will return at the **beginning of this Land Sabbath year** for the **first resurrection/rapture** and deliver YaHavah's wrath (his Great Tribulation), then the peaceful reign of Jesus on David's throne on earth for 1,000 years.

The prophecies for the first and second beasts were straightforward; they came to do what they needed to do and were finished. In order to understand Daniel's horrific vision of the Fourth Beast, we must first understand the third beast, its composition, and its purpose. There are four main prophecies and one sub-prophecy that funnel down to the entrance of the Fourth Beast.

Third Beast in Three Phases

Third Beast in Three Phases			
PHASE 1—Alexander the Great— Body of a leopard	333-323 BC (AM 4017-4027)		
PHASE 2—Four heads on the leopard	Alexander's four generals divide his Empire		
Lysimachus—Asia-Minor Cassander—Greece	Lysimachus and Cassander lost their portion to Rome in a very short time.		
Ptolomy—Egypt	323-30 BC (AM 4027-4320)	The Ptolemaic and Seleucid Empires fought for 260 years until the Seleucid Empire fell to Rome after the death of Antiochus IV Epiphanes (Daniel 11:3-28)	
Seleucus—Syria	323-63 BC (AM 4017-4287)		
The dragon with seven heads—five are fallen, and one is, [and] the other is not yet come; and when he comes, he must continue a short space (Revelation 17:10) Alexander and his four generals are fallen. One is Satan the spirit of the beast. The Fourth Beast is yet to come.			
PHASE 3—The Fourth Beast and his false prophet— Two sets of wings on the leopard	3.5 years	The Fourth Beast known as the Antichrist of the tribulation period will reign with terror, the last half of the last seven years—the last seven years of the final 49 years	

The third beast is complex because it includes other parts of prophecies in order to fulfill its purpose, such as the goat with one horn that changes to four horns and a little horn. It sounds confusing, but bear with me, and you will see how they all work together to reveal the Fourth Beast. Study Handbook 4, "Daniel's Four Beasts," contains the Book of Daniel and additional details on the four beasts.

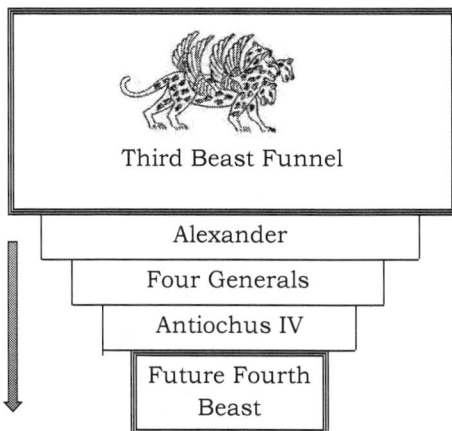

For now, the focus is only on the third beast. Its appearance is the body of a leopard, four heads, and two sets of wings. As you can see in the next image, this beast consists of three parts: the body (Alexander the Great), four heads (his four generals), and four wings, which are the Fourth Beast and his prophet.

The body of the leopard represents Alexander the Great whose time is finished. He came to bring in his four generals, which are the four heads and, also, the four horns on the goat who took over Alexander's kingdom when he died.

The four generals came and finished their purpose. A descendant of one of those generals, the fierce Seleucid Antiochus IV, (Epiphanes), came and died so that another fiercer than he could take his place far in the future.

This one will be the Fourth Beast, aka, the small sprout from one of the four horns on the goat that identifies the kingdom from which the Fourth Beast will come. He is also the small sprout on the dragon with ten horns, which identifies him with the ten toes on Nebuchadnezzar's statue and the ten nations around Israel with whom Israel played the harlot. The sprout is also one of the seven heads on the dragon.

As I said, it is complex, but understandable when all the parts are properly and biblically fitted together. Even a 1000-piece jigsaw puzzle is daunting when first dumped out on the table—but doable.

Nebuchadnezzar's colossus also plays a big part — no pun intended — in the parameters of prophecy interpretations and is included in my 4th prophecy handbook, *"Daniel's Fourth Beast."*

Care must be taken to not add to or take away from Bible prophecy. For example, many scholars believe the legs of Nebuchadnezzar's colossus represent Rome, but Rome is not mentioned in the description and prophecies of the third and Fourth Beast. The Preterist assumption that Rome is the Fourth Beast comes from an error made in interpreting Daniel 9:26 to mean the destruction of Jerusalem by Rome in AD 70. That verse is actually about the future time of the Fourth Beast in Jerusalem.

What is the answer to the riddle of the beast with seven heads which states, five were alive, one is, and one is yet to come? (Revelation 13:3) Briefly, what the Bible has shown us so far, the five are Alexander and his four generals; they were alive, now they are not. One is, stated this way, means not dead. The evil spirit of all four beasts is very much alive; he is Satan. The one who is yet to come is the small sprout from one of the horns (generals) on the goat. Again, common opinion says that Rome is the Fourth Beast; however, the sprout will come from the dead Seleucid Empire whose throne was in Syria. (Daniel 11:2-29)

Another common misconception is that the person to become the Antichrist will be killed and then resurrected from the dead. There is nothing in the Bible that specifically states the Antichrist (Fourth Beast) will be killed and resurrected. The Bible clearly indicates that Antiochus IV died in 63 AD and another will come in his place during the seventieth week of Daniel's prophecy. He will be many times worse than Antiochus IV (Epiphanes). Antiochus ordered a pig to be slain on the holy altar of sacrifice.

The Antichrist will violate the hearts of weak believers of Jesus Christ by taking the throne of YaHavah in their hearts. That is called apostacy. Maybe that is one reason this is called the Common Era—there are a lot of common notions that are not true to the Bible—*pun intended.* The prophecies of Ezekiel and Isaiah tell us that the third temple will be built during the millennial reign of Jesus; therefore, when the Antichrist is seen standing in the temple, it means the temple of the hearts of apostate believers.

Recap: Alexander and his four generals completed their time and died, but one like one of the four generals will come like a sprout on a dead stump, or as described by Daniel, a sprout out of one of the horns on the goat. (Daniel 8:9-14, 21-26)

Alexander the Great and his four generals are historical scenery events on Route 77. However, phase 3 of the third beast will sprout new life and come on the wings of abomination in the life of the Fourth Beast (Antichrist).

There are five connected end time Bible prophecies that provide a path through time and the tangle of historical people and events to the end. These five leave no room for assumptions and error. YaHavah tells us exactly what to look for and how to sift the information down to the final conclusion.

The signpost for the last seven years is the *seven-year agreement with many.* Then the sound of the first trumpet warning. With that trumpet warning, will come catastrophic forest fires consuming billions of acres of forest around the world in the first year. The world suffers horrendous forest fires every year, but this one beats all of them put together.

There will be no mistake of what is happening. If this does not happen in the last seven years in the 41st block—the block we are occupying right now—then we keep waiting and working to save more souls with the truth through the gospel of Jesus Christ. With global warming, there are increased frequency and intensity of earthquakes, and increased unrest between many nations, it is possible there is not much time left.

You can monitor the daily earthquakes worldwide at (http://earthquake.usgs.gov/earthquakes/map)

The linear road through the Bible is like a transparent tunnel. On the outside of the tunnel, history plays on the screen of time like a silent movie. Everyone takes an active part in the history of this world; however, only a remnant of the billions of souls born to this earth will declare their love of YaHavah with all their heart, mind, and soul. They are the ones who love, trust, and obey their Father in heaven. They will walk a sure road to the White Throne Judgment, while all the others stumble and stagger on paths in the forest beside the road only to end up in, well, you know where. A remnant is a portion less than the whole. Only YaHavah knows how many souls will remain written in the Book of Life from the beginning, for the Bible says the names of the disobedient will be blotted out of the Book for eternity. "Once saved always saved" is only true after Jesus returns.

All people, no matter what religious road they take, are headed in the same direction to meet at the Judgment Seat of Christ, aka, the White Throne Judgment. From there they go in different directions. Those whose names are in the Book of Life and whose heart intentions are for Father and Son will pass through the gate into New Jerusalem. Those whose heart intentions are far from Father and Son will spend eternity in a very hot climate far away from New Jerusalem.

Who are we going to call on for righteous counsel and understanding? What choices are we making that will decide whether our soul will respond to Jesus' call to meet him in the air at his second coming, or not?

Until that day, the road will continue with many opportunities for a change of heart. Life and its choices are more precious than gold and should not be squandered because after death those opportunities cease to exist.

Daniel's prophecy provides straightforward guidelines to follow. The Book of Revelation and other writing prophets fill in the details. Interpretation of all end-time prophecies from YaHavah must agree with the timing and word-parameters YaHavah placed in his prophecy of seventy-sevens combined with his coordinated prophecies. Additional guidelines in Bible hermeneutics are also helpful.

The simple end time statements of the seventy-sevens prophecy are meant to keep interpretation down to simple Bible knowledge and understanding.

If Christians listen to false teaching, as the majority do, transgressions against Father and Son will continue. YaHavah will not favor transgressing Christians any more than he has favored Israel in their transgressions. Transgression is transgression, sin is sin, and false teachings are lies against YaHavah and Jesus. Repeatedly, YaHavah sent his prophets to call the people back to him. Repeatedly, they would not listen, or they listened for only a short time and turned away again. Until Christians and Bible scholars start weeding out their doctrinal differences and turning to YaHavah for counsel and understanding, they will be treated no differently than any other sinner.

Recap: the kingdom of Judah was taken captive by Babylon for seventy years as was prophesied. This was their captivity. At the beginning of their captivity, the first temple in Jerusalem was destroyed by Nebuchadnezzar of Babylon. When Judah's seventy years of captivity was completed; so was the second temple rebuilt. The captives returned to Jerusalem, but their transgressions were not finished, nor were the transgressions of all humankind. But, praise the Lord, we have a door into the Kingdom of YaHavah. Jesus holds the key.

Daniel's prophecy of seventy-sevens is addressed to the tribes of Israel, but in the grace of YaHavah, it encompasses all peoples and nations for its full duration.

The next captivity will be for the tribes of Israel and her companions, the Gentiles, to finish the transgressions. Christians are considered as Gentiles by the Jews. At the end of this last captivity, the transgressions of Israel and all humankind will come to an end with the second coming of Jesus Christ and the sealing of the remnant of Israel in the Spirit of YaHavah to prepare them for the call of the first resurrection.

When he appears on a cloud for all to see, he will call all who are sealed in the Spirit of YaHavah, after which, he will deliver the wrath of YaHavah on all who are sealed in the seal of deceit, who is Satan. 666 is the number and seal of the sons of Adam.

The chronology of the Bible contains many people, genealogies, and events making it easy to get lost in the abundance of Bible and historical information. Many Bible scholars have tried to follow the entire chronology to the end but cannot get past the Babylonian captivity of Judah. However, the Bible, like a dense forest, has signs and a definite trail that leads past the Babylonian captivity all the way to New Jerusalem.

YaHavah promised the tribes of Israel he would deliver them one last time. Prophecy is about their redemption through Jesus Christ. By grace, the Gentiles who accept their Redeemer are included in their redemption and this fantastic journey to New Jerusalem.

What Are the Signs?

- Sabbath — the law and prophecy are based on Sabbath.

- Daniel's prophecy of seventy sevens is based on Sabbath.

- The order of King Cyrus for the rebuilding of the temple in Jerusalem started the countdown of Daniel's seventy sevens by Sabbaths.

- Jesus' first and second coming of Jesus is based on Sabbath and the three Feasts of YaHavah.

- The commandment to keep the Sabbath continues to the end. In other words, enter into YaHavah's rest. Honor the Sabbaths he set to lead us to the end.

- Daniel's description of the third beast reveals the mystery of the Fourth Beast.

- The only sign that begins the last seven years is the agreement with many for seven years then the first of seven trumpets.

- Ezekiel describes the building of the third temple during the millennial reign of Jesus, which will be a Land Sabbath year of (1,000-years)

One last item to consider is the sign that is not discussed in relation to the scroll with seven seals, which is the Book of Life. The scroll cannot be opened until the end of the millennium at the time of the White Throne Judgment, neither can the seventh-year end until the end of the millennium.

10—TABLE OF THE PROPHETS AND THEIR TIMES

The following table of prophets is arranged in the order of their time rather than the order they appear in most Bibles. Their books are also arranged in the Word of YHVH Bible in the order of their time.

BK #	PROPHETS	TO	KINGS	AM
31	Obadiah	Edom	Ahab, 3rd year; Ahaziah, and Joram	3543-3574
32	Jonah	Nineveh	pre Amaziah	pre-3561
30	Amos	Judah	Jeroboam II— 2 years before earthquake, Uzziah	3635-3662
28	Hosea	Judah/Israel	Jeroboam II, Uzziah, Jotham, Ahaz, Hezekiah	3676-3775
23	Isaiah	Judah/Israel	Uzziah, Jotham, Ahaz, Hezekiah	3714-3775
33	Micah	Judah	Jotham, Ahaz, Hezekiah	3715-3775
34	Nahum	Nineveh	Josiah, possibly in the reign of	3832-3863
36	Zephaniah	Judah	Josiah	3832-3863
24	Jeremiah	Judah	Josiah, 13th year to the 11th year of Zedekiah	3845-3885
35	Habakkuk	Judah	Jehoahaz, Jehoiakim	3863-3874

27	Daniel	Judah	Jehoiakim, 3rd year to 1st year of Darius	3866-3949
26	Ezekiel	Judah	Jehoiachin, 5th year of exile to the 27th year	3874-3900
25	Lamentations	Captivity	After destruction of Jerusalem	3885
37	Haggai	Judah	Darius, 2nd year of	3951
38	Zechariah	Judah	Darius, 2nd year of	3951
39	Malachi	Edom/Jacob	TRIBES OF ISRAEL	unknown
29	Joel	To the world	WORLD	unknown

The table for Sabbath year and Jubilee

SABBATH YEAR AND YEAR OF JUBILEE (Both are Land Sabbath)			
Sabbath Name	Duration	Time of Rest	Scripture
Land Sabbath	Sow for six years	7th year is rest for the land— no planting	Leviticus 25:1-7
Year of Jubilee	Seven Land Sabbaths or Forty-nine years from Passover	The 50th year is rest for the land—no planting	Leviticus 25:8-13

Letting the land rest every seventh year is good agricultural sense so the nutrients will not be used up. However, today's farmers are more likely to alternate crops and to fertilize the land.

The following table shows the three National Feasts

listed in the Bible before any other feasts were added. These are the Feasts that form the pattern for significant occurrences in the first and second coming of Jesus Christ.

THREE NATIONAL FEASTS OF YAHAVAH			
Feast Name	Month	Days	Scripture
Feast of Unleavened Bread, aka, Passover	1st month of the Sacred year. Begins 14th day of Nisan at twilight. (The time of the birth, baptism, and crucifixion of Jesus.)	Seven days	Exodus 23:14; Leviticus 23:5-8
Feast of the Harvest, aka, Feast of Weeks, and Pentecost	Seven Sabbaths from the end of Passover. The time of the pouring out of the seven spirits.	Begin on 50th day	Exodus 3:16; Leviticus 23:16
Feast of Ingathering, aka, Feast of Tabernacles, Feast of Booths	The seventh month of Sacred Year. 1st day of Tishri. Trumpets announce a Holy Convocation. The future timing of the return of Jesus	10th day— complete rest and humility before YHVH. The 15th day begins Feast	Leviticus 23:24-44

The timing for Jesus' conception, birth, baptism, death, ascension, and return is based on these Feasts. The seventy sevens are also connected to them and Sabbath.

The Jewish calendar is shown on the following page. Both, the Feasts and the calendar, are correlated to prophecies concerning the first and second coming of Jesus Christ.

Table of the Jewish Calendar

The Jewish day was from sunset to sunrise in eight equal parts: sunset to 9am; 9pm to midnight; midnight to 3am; 3am to sunrise; sunrise to 9am; 9am to noon; noon to 3pm; and 3pm to sunset.

Hebrew months are alternately 30 and 29 days long. Their year had 354 days. About every 3 years (7 times in 19 years) an extra 29-day month, VEADOR, was added between ADAR and NISAN.

The Jews use two calendars:
Civil Calendar— official calendar of kings, childbirth, and contracts.
Sacred Calendar— used to compute festivals
Everything about Jesus and end time prophecy is also connected to the Sacred Calendar.

Month Name	Corresponds with:	No. of days	Month of Civil Year	Month of Sacred Year
TISHRI	Sept/Oct 3rd—Feast of Ingathering announced by trumpets. **Return of Jesus**	30	1	7
HESHVAN	Oct/Nov	29 or 30	2	8
CHISLEV	Nov/Dec	29 or 30	3	9
TEBETH	Dec/Jan	29	4	10
SHEBAT	Jan/Feb	30	5	11
ADAR	Feb/Mar	29 or 30	6	12
NISAN or ABIB	Mar/Apr 1st—*Feast of Passover* **Birth, anointing, and crucifixion of Jesus**	30	7	1
IYAR	Apr/May 2nd—*Feast of Pentecost* **Christ glorified and seven spirits sent out**	29	8	2
SIVAN	May/June	30	9	3
TAMMUZ	June/July	29	10	4
AB	July/Aug	30	11	5
ELUL	Aug/Sept	29	12	6

11—CHRONOLOGICAL ORDER OF THE BIBLE

The following is a synopsis of the timing and events previously shown.

It is important to understand Bible timelines because they are YaHavah's parameters to keep us within his plan. The serious Bible student must become familiar with the chronology of the main people and events of the Bible related to Jesus' genealogy and end time prophecies. The previous ten sections provide Bible-based linear calendar (AM) for counting the years from Adam to the end is far more useful than the current Gregorian method of BC and AD.

(AM 130-2239) people in Jesus' genealogy. This portion takes us from Adam who at age 130 fathered Seth, to Jacob (Israel) who by the age 130 had fathered twelve sons known as the twelve tribes of Israel and began an extended stay of 430 years in Egypt.

(AM 2239-2709) time of Egyptian captivity and Wilderness journey of the twelve tribes of Israel (Jacob) (Genesis 14:17 through Exodus 1:1—40:38)

(AM 2709-3362) time of Judges over the tribes and their wavering between righteous judges and oppression (Joshua 1:1-1Samuel 8:1-22) It is here that the Jewish Masoretic scholars fell short in their chronological timing from Adam.

(AM 3362-3482) time of the United Kingdom of the twelve tribes with King Saul, King David, and King Solomon (1Samuel 9:1 through 1Kings 11:43)

(AM 3482-3752) time of the split kingdom of Israel in the North (ten tribes in Syria) and Judah in the South (two tribes in Jerusalem) to the fall of Israel and dispersion of the ten tribes (1Kings 11:42 through 2Kings 17:6)

(AM 3746-3885) the beginning of the fall of Jerusalem (2Kings 18:1 through 2Kings 25:1-8)

This begins the time of Daniel's prophecy of four great beasts in Daniel chapters 7, 8, and 11.

(The asterisks ** below mark fulfilled prophecies)

(AM 3885-3932) Babylonian captivity began with Nebuchadnezzar (first beast—the lion). Later, Cyrus (first king of the second beast—the bear) issued a decree to **restore Jerusalem (Daniel 9:24-25; Isaiah 44:24-28) and the temple which was completed in 3955 (Ezra 6:1) also completing the Babylonian captivity of seventy years from 3885-3955. Darius I (second king of the second beast) reissues Cyrus' decree after a long delay.

The total captivity was from AM 3885-3932. The question has come up—is it the captivity in Babylon or the captivity of Babylon? Jerusalem was allowed to have its kings of Judah over Jerusalem, but Babylonian kings ruled over Judah's kings and the land. YaHavah uses the title of "Babylon, the mother of harlots" to represent the captivity of the perpetual sin of Adam through every father. It is also refers to the pollution of the throne in Jerusalem beginning with Solomon and the beginning of the four beasts of Daniel. The reason is that sin against YaHavah. The people of Jerusalem did not give full honor to YaHavah through the celebration of the three Feasts of YHVH which are based on agricultural seasons and Sabbaths (resting in YaHavah on the seventh day, seventh year, and fiftieth year). Joel cried out because honor to YaHavah was taken away from the people during captivity. The end time Fourth Beast will do the same and more.

12—PROPHECIES WITHIN YHVH's SEVENTY SEVENS

These are the parameters within YaHavah's calendar. They are his interpretation fences to corral the imaginations of men and hold them in check and to test the spirit of all doctrines to see if they are of YaHavah.

(** indicates fulfilled prophecy)

(AM 3932-3980) the first period of seventy-sevens; a 49-year block of **Seven Land Sabbaths; **Artaxerxes I (third king of the second beast) issues a decree to restore Jerusalem's wall in 3936 four years after YaHavah's calendar of time to the end began. (Daniel 9:25; Nehemiah 2:1, 6:15, 8:1-18)

(AM 3981-4414) the second period of seventy-sevens is ** Sixty-Two Land Sabbaths to **make atonement for iniquity and **anoint the Most Holy or anointing of Jesus at his baptism. (See AM 4412)

(AM 4017—4027) The first phase of the third Beast of Daniel's prophecy is Alexander the Great (333-323 BC) the beast with the body of a leopard with four heads and two sets of wings on its back.

(AM 4027—4087) The second phase of the third Beast of Daniel is the four heads on the leopard representing Alexander's four generals who divided his kingdom among them. (Daniel 11)

(AM 4381) **Jesus' birth

The birth of Jesus is often referred to as the incarnation of God into human form. The incarnation of a god into a human form is a remnant of paganism and of the Hellenization of Jews and Christians throughout their history. Jesus did not exist

The doctrine of incarnation disavows every truth and purpose of Jesus' sinless conception and birth.

before his birth, except in the mind of YaHavah for salvation from and destruction of sin. The Bible says the heavens and earth were created for him. He said he was *sent from above* because his father is the highest authority in all creation. He came from above because his father is in heaven, not part of the created earth. All other humans come from below because Adam was created from the elements of the earth.

The sin of Adam was passed on and perpetuated through every father from beginning to end. (Genesis 3:1-24) Jesus is the only exception because he did not have a human father. His biological father is YaHavah Elohim, and his mother is in the line of King David of Judah, giving him birthrights to the Kingdom of YaHavah and Judah's throne of David. Mary, his mother, was of the line of Judah through David's son Nathan, not Solomon. (Luke 3:31) His birthright to the Kingdom of YaHavah was fulfilled when he ascended to heaven to be glorified. (Revelation 5:5-7) His earthly stepfather, Joseph, was of the cursed line of Judah through Solomon (Matthew 1:6), providing two more reasons why Joseph or any human could not be the biological father of Jesus. The first reason is that the sin of Adam is perpetuated through every human father to his offspring. Jesus broke that chain for all who believe in and accept what he did on the cross in our stead.

> *The current pre, mid, and post tribulationist doctrines that say all seven seals on the scroll with seven seals represents the last seven years disavows every truth and purpose of all prophecy.*

(AM 4412) **Jesus is anointed in the Spirit (Isaiah 11:1-2—tells us what the anointing is; Daniel 9:24—prophesied the anointing of the Holy One; Matthew 3:11-16—the anointing was fulfilled)

(AM 4415) **after sixty-two sevens, Jesus died on the cross, was resurrected from the grave, and ascended to his throne in heaven between Passover and Pentecost in the first month of the first year of the chronological seventieth week.

Jesus ascended into heaven to receive the Book of Life, better known as the scroll with seven seals, and to release the anointing of the seven spirits also known as the promised Comforter. (Revelation 5:6; Acts 2:1-4—fulfilled in the rebirth and regeneration of believers)

False prophets will suffer the wrath of YaHavah with all who follow their false teaching. It's enough to scare me, and to fear YaHavah (have a deeper respect for him and what he can do).

The seven seals of the scroll with seven seals is about the choices between good and evil before the scroll opens to reveal the names remaining in the Book of Life—the choices are the truth of YaHavah or the deception of Satan. Only the sixth and seventh seals represent the occurrences of the last seven years in which choices between good and evil remain.

(AM—unknown—the end appointed by YaHavah) This is the time of the third period of seven years, or one Land Sabbath, and the third phase of the third Beast.

Only two of Alexander's generals survived—Seleucus of Syria and Ptolemy of Egypt. (Daniel 11:1-28) At its appointed time in the last seven years, a small sprout will bring new life into the Syrian Empire that died in 63 BC. (Daniel 11:29-42)

The doctrine that claims the last seven years occurred in 70 AD with the destruction of the Temple in Jerusalem by Rome disavows every Bible prophecy concerning the second coming of Christ and all of the prophecies of the seventieth week; all because of the misinterpretation of one short phrase in Daniel *9:26b.*

This one false doctrine has given birth to a plethora of false doctrine, and it started with both Calvin and Luther. Consider this. If the seventieth week is finished, Jesus will not be seen returning on a cloud, there will be no sealed remnant of Israel as promised by YaHavah, no millennial reign of

66

Jesus Christ, Satan will never be chained for a thousand years or destroyed, sin cannot be destroyed, and no White Throne Judgment. These are all prophecies that cannot happen if the last seven years was finished in the first century. Another major consideration is that John did not write the Book of Revelation until sometime in the AD 90s after the destruction of the Temple by Rome.

The seventieth week must occur at an appointed time in the future for the remaining prophecies to occur at their appointed times. The human condition can neither speed it up nor slow it down. It is totally dependent on YaHavah's timing.

Let me clarify. Some preterists are saying we must take dominion and bring all people to the saving knowledge of Jesus Christ <u>before he can return</u>. A person in Simi Valley, California repeatedly contacted me with this outrageous lie, and he would not even begin to consider that he was in error. He is completely deluded and passes his delusions off as truth. He is older than me, so, unless he changed his teaching to the truth, he may have died with false doctrine burned into his soul with the mark of 666.

Believe the Bible and listen to the Spirit of YaHavah. Fear YaHavah.

Future Prophecies to be fulfilled at a Time Only Known to YHVH

Perhaps a bit of fine tuning with regard to Bible terminology is in order for the remainder of this section.

Tribulation and Tribulation Period is defined as forms of *affliction, distress, trials*, and *oppression*. From Adam until now, man has always known *tribulation*. From its inception,

> *It is a common error to call the time of the Antichrist the Great Tribulation. However, to attribute the biblical term Great Tribulation to the Antichrist is to change the meaning and purpose of the anger of YaHavah.*

the Church has always known *tribulation*. The end time tribulation period is the last seven years of Daniel's prophecy. It is a testing period for everyone who is alive when it begins, much like the last shaking and cleaning of grain.

YaHavah causes all of the signs of the seven trumpets during the tribulation period. How they are viewed depends on which side of the line of demarcation the people are on. The tribulation of 1,290 days caused by the Fourth Beast will be added to the time of testing from YaHavah.

Great tribulation, aka, wrath of YHVH

Matthew 24:20-22 *20–But pray that your flight be not in the winter, neither on the Sabbath day: 21–for then shall be great tribulation, (Rev. 6:17)* **such as was not since the beginning of the world to this time, nor ever shall be after it.** *22–And except those days should be shortened, there should no flesh be saved: but for the elect's sake those days shall be shortened.*

Do not mistake the great tribulation of Matthew 24:21 as from the Antichrist of the last seven years. The tribulation he causes cannot surpass that of the wrath of YaHavah, whose wrath this time will be greater than the flood or destruction of Sodom and Gomorrah. Never has YaHavah poured out a greater wrath than when he destroys sin altogether in the end. In verse 29 it states the Son of Man will be seen *after the tribulation of that time* (the first six years) and describes all of the signs of the end. Jesus calls the Saints out of harm's way under the sign of returning on a cloud, then delivers the seven bowls of wrath that is the great tribulation mentioned in verse 21 under the sign of the king on a white horse. This correlates with Revelation 2:21-23; 6:17; 7:13-17.

Great Tribulation is the wrath of YaHavah which is the anger of YaHavah poured out on the Antichrist and all sinners. This is when the son of perdition will be revealed for who he really is, but too late for those who took his mark. Again, 666 means they are permanently marked as sons of Adam. But what does that mark mean?

The number, 666, has a Bible answer within Bible context related to the creation and fall of man. The man, Adam, was created and fell to sin on the **sixth day** of creation. On the seventh day, YaHavah rested. He will rest again in the seventh day of Daniel's last seven years during the millennium. The **sixth of the seven spirits** of YaHavah is knowledge; its opposite in the spirit of lawlessness is **ignorance**. All sinful mankind will be destroyed at the end of the **sixth year** (trumpet) described on the scroll with seven seals in the Book of Revelation.

666	In the Spirit of YHVH	In the spirit of lawlessness (sin)
6th day	Creation of man	Fall of man
6th spirit	Knowledge of the truth of YHVH and Jesus	Ignorance and turning away from the truth of YHVH and Jesus
6th year, end of	Resurrection of Saints	Destruction of sinful sons of Adam

Those who take the mark of the Beast during his horrendous reign do not recognize him as the Antichrist. When Jesus appears on a cloud, he will be revealed for who and what he is. He and his false prophet will be cast into the pit of fire forever. These two will "not pass go" to the White Throne Judgment.

The Bible is clear that the last seven years is a time of tribulation and the wrath of YaHavah is the Great Tribulation, aka, indignation, time of trouble, and 7 bowls of

YaHavah's wrath. Understanding the difference is extremely important to the process of interpretation and prevention of being caught in Satan's web of deceit.

Notice the difference between the use of the word *tribulation* in Matthew 24:20-22 and 24:29. The Bible is YaHavah's thoughts, words, and intents. We must pay attention to every word.

Matthew 24:15-19— *15—When you, therefore, shall see the abomination of desolation, spoken of by Daniel the prophet, stand in the holy place, (whoso reads, let him understand:) 16—then let them which be in Judaea flee into the mountains: 17—let him which is on the housetop not come down to take anything out of his house: 18— neither let him which is in the field return back to take his clothes. 19—And woe to them that are with child, and to them that give suck in those days!*

In other words, those who have not taken the mark of the beast and are left behind, run for your lives because the Great Day of YaHavah has arrived. The abomination of desolation is about to be destroyed.

Great tribulation, aka, wrath of YHVH

(continued)— *20—But pray that your flight is not in the winter, neither on the Sabbath day: 21—for then shall be **great tribulation, such as was not since the beginning of the world to this time, nor ever shall be after it.** 22—And except those days should be shortened, there should no flesh be saved: but for the elect's sake those days shall be shortened.*

Again, consider this—Verse 21 says the world has never before seen the extent of YaHavah's end-time wrath and it will never see it again. Giving the distinction of "Great Tribulation" to the last Antichrist is very short-sighted.

Matthew 24:29-31— *29—Immediately after the tribulation of those days shall the sun be darkened, and the moon shall not give her light, and the stars shall fall from heaven, and the powers of the heavens shall be shaken: 30—and then shall appear the sign of the Son of man in heaven: and then shall all the tribes of the earth mourn, and they shall see the Son of man coming in the clouds of heaven with power and great glory. 31—And he shall send his angels with a great sound of a trumpet, and they shall gather together his elect from the four winds, from one end of heaven to the other.*

The phrase, *after the tribulation,* means at the end of the Antichrist's reign of terror and the signs of each of the first six trumpets.

The Order in Which the Last Prophecies Will Occur

PROPHECY 1: the making of a seven-year agreement with many made by the man who will become the Fourth Beast, aka, Antichrist, and Abomination of desolation (Daniel 9:26b-27)

PROPHECY 2: the last seven years to be fulfilled which are described in the seventh seal (Revelation 8:1—11:19) of the scroll with seven seals and in several OT prophecies

PROPHECY 3: The third phase of the third Beast of Daniel's prophecy of four beasts.

This is the Fourth Beast and his false prophet represented by the two sets of wings on the third Beast's body. His appointed time is in the last 3.5 years of the first six years. This will fulfill the coming of the Antichrist of the last seven years of Daniel's seventy sevens. He is also the little horn sprouting from one of the four horns on the goat of Daniel and the little horn sprouting from one of the tens

71

horns on the beast of Revelation. (Daniel 7:7-8; Revelation 13:1-18) Daniel provides key characteristics of the Antichrist.

Daniel 11:36-37— *36—And the king shall do according to his will, and he shall exalt himself, and magnify himself above every god, and shall speak harsh things against the God (El) of gods, and shall prosper until the indignation be accomplished: for that which is determined shall be done. 37—Neither shall he regard the god of his fathers, nor the desire of women, nor regard any god: for he shall magnify himself above all.*

The indignation is YaHavah's seven bowls of wrath described in Revelation 15:1—16:21, also called the Great Tribulation in Matthew 24:20-22; Revelation 2:21-23, 7:13-15. It is also marked by the revealing of the Abomination of Desolation of Matthew 24:15 and Mark 13:14.

Why was it important to prophesy that this man has no desire for women? Here are two Bible reasons for these character traits which are probably one reason the Fourth Beast distressed Daniel so much.

The man called the Fourth Beast, Antichrist, and Abomination of desolation will be a combination of everything YaHavah hates. He will perform the pagan craft such as was done in the time of Noah that caused the Great Flood and the homosexual behavior in the time of Abraham that caused the destruction of Sodom and Gomorrah. Will he keep these flaws secret until he gains a strong alliance and power? Or is his lack of desire for women an Islamic trait?

Putting all of Daniel's prophecies of the four beasts together reveals to us that the Antichrist and his prophet are the four wings on the back of the leopard called the Third Beast and the lower part of the legs of Nebuchadnezzar's colossus.

PROPHECY 4: Ministry and death of two prophets of YaHavah in the last 3.5 years of the first six years (Revelation 11:3-13)

The last seven years cannot end until the end of the millennium and sin is destroyed by the final destruction of Satan. The seventh year (Land Sabbath) is one thousand years long and reserved for the millennial reign of Christ on the earth. It sounds impossible until we read:

2Peter 3:8-9— 8—*But, beloved, be not ignorant of this one thing, that one day [is], with our Adonai, as a thousand years, and a thousand years as one day.* 9—*Adonai is not slack concerning his promise, as some men count slackness; but is patient toward us, not willing that any should perish, but that all should come to repentance.*

This truth is hidden in the bright light of YaHavah's Spirit because darkness does not comprehend his light.

PROPHECY 5: The 144,000 remnant of the twelve tribes of Israel will be hidden from the Beast and nurtured for 3.5 years. (Revelation 12:6, 15-17; Joel 2:21-24)

PROPHECY 6: The twelve tribes of Israel (144,000 remnant) will receive Jesus and the anointing in the Spirit of YaHavah per his promise of a second remnant. (Isaiah 11:11-12; Joel 2:28-29; Revelation 6:12—7:17, 12:13-14)

The first was their exodus from Egypt. The timing of their last exodus is moments before the seventh trumpet sounds, and Jesus appears on a cloud. The image is also of Jesus standing on the split Mountain to enter Azal. (Zechariah 14:5) The Red Sea was split for the Israelites to cross out of Egypt, but the Mount will be split for the second departure of the twelve tribes out of Babylon the Great, Mother of Harlots as a sea of sinners — theirs and humanity's transgressions against YaHavah.

The context in which the Hebrew word *Azal* is used may be associated with the Day of Atonement when sin will end forever. Azal has several meanings, one of which is, *join.* In the context used by Zechariah and the split mountain of Revelation, it means "to go up." This is the time of the resurrection when the saints and remnant will be called to meet Jesus in the air at the beginning of the Great Day of YHVH before His wrath is poured out.

PROPHECY 7: Jesus descends on a cloud to call and remove the saints from the harm of the wrath of YaHavah, aka, Great Tribulation, which is YaHavah's indignation, wrath, and time of trouble as described by Joel and referenced in Mark 24:21. The resurrected (changed saints from nearly 7,000 years of history and the remnant of Israel) will be held in a safe place until the wrath is complete.

The turnaround action of the resurrected is also a misconception of the pre, mid, and post-tribulation rapture teachings. The current pre and post-trib premillennial teachings also hold a false understanding of the scroll with seven seals.

Participants in the first resurrection will not be present or take part in delivering the seven bowls of YaHavah's wrath. (Revelation 15:1-8; Isaiah 26:20)

The return of Christ is post-tribulation and premillennial under YaHavah's purpose and understanding of the scroll. It is a misconception of the first four seals that is the cause of serious misinterpretation of the scroll. See book number 2 in this series "The Scroll with Seven Seals."

PROPHECY 8: Jesus then descends to earth as the king on a white horse to deliver the seven bowls of YaHavah's wrath, aka, Armageddon and destruction of the Antichrist and all bearing his mark. (Revelation 19:1-20)

PROPHECY 9: Satan is chained and thrown into the pit for 1000 years (Revelation 20:1-3)

PROPHECY 10: Those who last 1,335 days are the survivors of the wrath who neither took the "mark of the Beast" nor was anointed in the Spirit of YaHavah. Those who set on the fence like roosting hens will be "left behind" at the long-awaited call to "Come up here." They will live and procreate during the millennium. (Daniel 12:8-13) The resurrected/raptured saints cannot procreate. They are like the angels who never marry. Marriage implies procreation.

PROPHECY 11: The millennial reign of Jesus on earth (Revelation 20:4-6)

PROPHECY 12: YaHavah said he would not share his mount with any other. The Muslim Mosque will have been destroyed during YaHavah's wrath, and the House of YaHavah (third temple) will be built on a clean temple mount for Jesus to sit on the throne of David during his millennial reign on earth. The building of the Third Temple and assigning of the land to the twelve tribes of Israel is described in Ezekiel chapters 37—48.

PROPHECY 13: The millennium ends with the release of Satan and war of Gog/Magog—this is how the survivors of the wrath will be sifted before the Book of Life is opened. There will be no dividing line between nations or religious denominations during the millennium. All peoples will be one nation under YaHavah and Jesus. (Revelation 20:7-10; Ezekiel 38:1-14)

PROPHECY 14: The second resurrection is the second death for all who do not accept the whole truth of the first and second coming of Jesus Christ (Revelation 20:11-15)

PROPHECY 15: The White Throne Judgment will take place when Jesus has finished breaking the seven seals, and the Book of Life is opened for judgment. Remember that the seven seals are about choices between good and evil expressed in different ways. (Revelation 20:11-15 and many other references)

The end of one beginning and

the beginning of another for eternity.

Pray for the knowledge of YaHavah's

truth to spread around the world and

for the salvation of many.

ABOUT THE AUTHOR

Mary E Lewis, an online-published author for more than twenty years, believes that "one mind in the Spirit" means there should be no diverse doctrines and Bible disagreements among faithful Christians. Her goal in Christian writing is to bring each reader into a deeper personal relationship with YaHavah by being of one mind and heart in the Spirit of YaHavah through the shed blood of Jesus Christ.

Ms. Lewis believes her real education is in 37 years of training in YaHavah's Word after the age of 40. Her path to her ministry in YaHavah's Word was long. When she was 10 years old, YaHavah answered a simple prayer asking what she could do to serve him. He told her that healing would come through her hands. She didn't understand, but she believed him. When she was 25, the angel of the Lord showed her the reason for YaHavah's promise. She again didn't understand but believed. When she was 40, she learned the reality of YaHavah's greatest opponent of His promises and received Jesus Christ as her Lord and Savior. Ms. Lewis is confident that YaHavah's promise to a child of 10 will ultimately bring many to a deeper understanding of the grace of YaHavah, Jesus Christ, and end time prophecy freeing them from the deadly words of false prophets in shepherds clothing.

The Grace of YaHavah and of Jesus Christ be with your spirit.

Books by Mary E. Lewis

Follow me to get updates at
amazon.com/author/mary_e_lewis

- Word of YHVH Bible: Discovering a Familiar Friend (Introduction to the Bible)
- Word of YHVH Bible: Glossary of Bible Terms
- Creation, Law, and History: Word of YHVH Bible Volume 1 (in paperback)
- Israel's Poetry and Prophets: Word of YHVH Bible Volume 2 (in paperback)
- New Testament: Word of YHVH Bible Volume 3 (in paperback)
- Word of YHVH Bible: Old Testament (complete in eBook format only)
- Word of YHVH Bible: New Testament (complete in eBook format only)
- Seven Spirits, Seven Lamps, Seven Churches
- The Scroll with Seven Seals
- Daniel's Four Beasts
- The Revelation of Jesus Christ: Vol. 1 The Writing on the outside of the scroll
- The Revelation of Jesus Christ: Vol. 2 The Writing on the inside of the scroll (focus on Book of Life)
- Why Jesus Had to be Human
- The Invisible Bridge (focus on understanding Father, Son, and Spirit)

Other titles are listed on my author page:
amazon.com/author/mary_e_lewis
website: www.fireofthelord.com
Copy and paste into your browser.

81278358R00046

Made in the USA
Lexington, KY
13 February 2018